Good Sounds Easy

Digital Production Sound for
Micro-Budget Filmmakers

Jeremy F. Crowson

DEDICATION

For Evan and Claire, so they might understand why and where I go with crates of equipment they help me to load, and for Donna, who tolerates my absence and ambition because she understands the "why" already.

CONTENTS

Acknowledgments

ACKNOWLEDGMENTS

Thank you to Chuck Hartsell, the first person who asked me to transfer my experience in sound to the field of filmmaking. Also to Andrew Bellware, who has given both advice and humor when needed during my quest to learn this mysterious craft. To a great Director of Photography, David Brower, who imparted much on-set wisdom to me, whether he meant to or not. And thank you to so many others who have trusted me with their projects. I value each and have learned from them all.

1 INT. THE SETUP - DAY

As a sound mixer for low-budget indie films I often run into the same scenario. It plays out something like this:

> DIRECTOR
> Hey, man, can you come run sound for us on this short next weekend? We have equipment; we just need someone who knows how to use it.

> ME
> I think I can make time. What equipment do you have?

> DIRECTOR
> We have an H4n and a shotgun mic. Oh, and I've got some headphones, too.

> ME
> Um, okay. What's the shoot? Interiors? Exteriors? Any action? What's the

environment?

DIRECTOR
It's all interiors. Mostly large rooms
with high ceilings. The acoustics sound
great!

Who found all the problems in this conversation?

First, to be sure, the little Zoom H4n is not one
of the problems. Almost any digital recorder with
XLR inputs will do nowadays, for basic micro-budget
production sound with a single mic. It's not even the
borrowed headphones, which I never use for three
reasons: I know how things are supposed to sound
through my own headphones, so it makes me more
reliable at capturing good sound; the headphones
directors have are usually not very good; and it's kind
of gross, like sharing lip balm.

The problems above stem from the notions that
most non-sound-guys seem to have on movie sets:
that a shotgun mic is what you need to capture good
sound, regardless of situation, and that a pleasant
sounding room will make the audio sound nice.

A room having "good acoustics" to the ears
means it will be a virtual nightmare for the sound guy.
Plus, a heavy reverb (a.k.a. good acoustics) interior is
the exact wrong place to use a shotgun mic.

Confused? Think I must be nuts? Your film-set
on-the-job training tells you that when a room is
echo-y you need to focus the mic tightly on the
actors' mouths to reduce the ambient reverb, which
means you should use a very tight shotgun mic, right?
After all, what other type of microphone is there for

movie production? Shotgun = Movie! Right?

NO. If the previous paragraph applies to you, then you definitely need to keep reading. You are why I'm writing this. Let's be clear: I am not writing this to talk down to you or overload you with tech jargon and calculations, but rather to re-educate all of you non-sound-guys, camera-jockeys, and micro-budget directors on what it takes to get decent production sound, because I find so many of you with incorrect information that has permeated your group, and everyone thinks it's right. So even if you think you know sound ... keep reading. There's a good chance you'll discover that at least part of what you take to be a given about production sound is very, very wrong.

In this short text, we will discuss microphones, digital audio recorders (a.k.a. field recorders), cables, headphones, boom-poles, wind and noise suppression, power, wired and wireless lavalieres, file formats, mic placement and techniques, and even touch on mixing boards and how to think about post-production sound while you're in production and why that's important. Also included is a short scenario guide to help you quickly evaluate a scene and situation to capture the best audio possible.

What we will **not** discuss in this text: overly complex audio tech, any mathematical calculations, and other B.S. that typically turns audio how-to books into a foreign language for anyone not already educated in audio.

I was skimming an "intro to film audio" book (always look for good tips ... never stop learning.) when the idea for this simple little book hit me.

ME
How is this an "intro" book? If I didn't
already know what the hell they're
talking about, it would be like trying to
read Portuguese!

At which point I was reminded of a blog post in
which the author lamented the complexities of
production audio, and dreamed of new tech that
would make it easier for non-sound-guys. I think I
may have pissed him off with my comments,
inadvertently, by suggesting that some of his ideas
wouldn't be possible. I certainly liked the general
concept, and found many of his ideas to be good, and
probably marketable if the artificial intelligence
required could be developed. Obviously he knew
audio - or at least the problems associated with
production audio - better than the average camera-
jockey, but the core conundrum seemed to persist.
"Why is good film sound so hard?"
Then it occurred to me: 99% of people I've run
across in small indie crews have been told how to run
sound by people who themselves had bad
information. It's a long chain of misinformation and
accidental ignorance that has made ultra-low-budget
movie crews think that sound is either some great
mystery that can only be unraveled by going to
recording-engineer school, or that it's all a hoax in its
complexity and all you need is a cheap hand-held
recorder, a cheap shotgun mic, and a production
assistant to hold the boom and press the record
button.
The reality is that it falls somewhere between
those two. Fortunately, however, today's current

technology leaves it closer to the latter ... if you have accurate information in your head of what the sound equipment can do, how to use it, and what is and isn't important.

2 INT. YOUR MOTIVATION - DAY

So why do you need good quality sound? Simple: your movie sucks without it. It has been said time and again that 70% of the audience experience when watching a movie falls on the sound. Granted, much of the sound-scape experience comes from the sound design, or effects, and musical score. However, at the core of it all lays the dialog track. If all other elements are great, but the audience can't hear or understand what the actors are saying, or if it's riddled with thumps, scrapes, too much reverberation, too much ambient noise, or if any of it doesn't blend well, it will yank the audience out of the experience quicker than seeing the worst rendered CGI monster imaginable.

Sound is important. So how do you make sure you capture good, clean dialog? Short of hiring me or some other experienced audio geek, many of whom are overpaid, though most (ahem) rarely get paid at all, you'll need to have someone on set dedicated to working sound - if possible. This person will be the sound department. He will be largely ignored by the rest of the crew and actors. He will carry a large part of your movie on his back alone, so he must be reliable. He must be able to adapt to any situation and be a quick, creative problem solver. He must be able to tolerate having the director of photography yelling at him that the boom is in frame ... repeatedly. Pick someone, and give them this book. If that someone is you, don't worry. It's not as hard as most people think.

First, let's change how you think. This is probably the hardest step. It begins with the script and preparing for the shoot, boiling down to the not so simple questions: What equipment do you need? How do you best use it?

To be able to answer these questions, for any movie, you need to understand the equipment and what it can do. The first core element of that equation is to understand microphones, their various applications, and how to use them correctly. I will not be going into advanced tech detail, as I said. However, you will get a solid understanding of what types of microphones are used in film production on location, and how best to use the various standard types to attain the best results for your project. Study thoroughly. Your director will thank you later. If you're the director, you'll thank yourself during post.

Aside from understanding the equipment, you need to know what to record and what to avoid. It's not always as obvious as you may think. Using equipment effectively is not just about what setting to punch in to the recorder, or where to hold the mic. Skill in recording audio means that you must constantly be thinking, and understanding one thing: production audio only needs to sound clean. Meaning, no garbage or unwanted noise in the recording, while being able to clearly hear what you intended to record – typically the actors' voices. This task is vastly more difficult than most people realize. However, with the right knowledge in your cranium, it's vastly easier than most people with *wrong* knowledge think it is. Confused? No? Ready to learn the right way to do it?

Okay, on with it then…build the foundation…

3 INT. THE BASICS - DAY

Similar to storyboarding or planning your shot list, with audio you must first know what you need to accomplish. Once you have your goal, then you can figure out how to achieve it. Like planning a shot list, planning for location audio begins with reading the script.

SCRIPT ANALYSIS

As you read each scene, try to imagine the physical layout. If you're reading a shooting script this will be much easier, as every shot will already be described. Remember, however, that directors and D.P.'s can and often do change things like that on a whim. Be ready for variations.

The majority of shots can easily be handled with standard equipment. What you must watch for are the oddball shots. Do you have a shot with six people speaking almost at once as they move around a room? Do you have a shot with gunfire? These types of situations you'll need to know about in advance, and be prepared. The majority of special situations will simply require you to know what mic to use and how.

SO, YOU'VE GOT MONO ...

Yes, mono, as in monaural. For movies, you do not need to record in stereo. Stereo and surround panning will be done in post-production. Dialog tracks go front and center. Keep it simple during production. Even if you have multiple mics recording at once and find yourself loading up an eight track recorder, each of those eight tracks will be recorded in mono and separately definable through the broadcast wave file (.BWF) that most recorders use.

WHAT SOUNDS DO YOU WANT?

There are only three types of sounds you will need to record on set. And most people would limit this to two. I have found that in micro-budget work, and especially if doing something fast, like a time limited competition, I prefer three.

Dialog – Duh.

Room Tone – Room Tone, Room Tone! Did I mention room tone? Room tone is simple. Tell everyone to shut up for a minute while you record, with gain cranked up, 20 to 30 seconds or more of the room you've just shot in, only now with nothing going on. You'll need this in post. If you have an experienced post audio dialog editor, he or she will flog you with your boompole if you come home with no room tone.

Room Tone is just what it sounds like: the tone (sound) the room makes, all by itself. Every room sounds different, with a different natural reverb and different ambient elements that you don't really notice most of the time. But this natural tone is what will blend your different dialog takes and tracks together and make everything sound as if it was recorded in one continuous take.

That said, "room" tone isn't only for rooms. Record the ambient sound wherever you record, even outside on a busy street. You'll thank me later, and your dialog editor will love you for it. Record the room tone with everyone and everything that was there during the shot, otherwise the "tone" is compromised and won't match exactly. Anyone who speaks or moves during recording of tone is subject to a smack in the head by the assistant director (who should be just as adamant as you about getting the tone recorded).

Wild Sounds – These are what I often refer to as "live Foley," and this is the stuff that most people don't think is necessary. I have found catching these sounds supremely valuable. So even if the director says it's an MOS shot (a mysterious abbreviation that means "without sound"), always roll sound on every take if you can manage it. Even if you're just shooting a cardioid across the center of the room, or have a shotgun aimed at someone's feet as they walk across a patch of gravel, these sounds can make life much easier when editing. Sometimes they're not usable. That's okay too. Better to have them than to not.

Another aspect of wild sounds to consider is the "instant ADR" that sometimes is a very valuable tool in post-production. If you're not sure you caught an actor's lines clean, then immediately after the scene has wrapped take the actor to a quiet area and have him run his lines again, trying to match the dynamics from the scene. If the director had him say the lines a few different ways, he should try to match whatever he did while the cameras were rolling. I have used the wild dialog tracks more than once in post.

SOUNDS TO AVOID

Obviously there will also be some sounds and noises you don't want to record. Most of these will occur during the recording of dialog, and there is often nothing you can do to make them go away. Therefore you must minimize their effect on the recording.

Air Conditioners – For a location sound man, air conditioning (or central heating) is a bane straight from hell. If possible, turn it off during the shot. If you can't turn it off, you'll have to minimize its impact by adjusting the low cut filter on the recorder and/or mic - typically to a higher setting, reducing the gain setting on the recorder, and bringing the mic closer to the actors' mouths. Testing the directionality of the mic to see if recording from one direction or another helps to minimize the volume of the air conditioner is also a simple trick. In other words, move the mic around to different places while still aiming it at the actor and see if you suddenly don't hear the a/c as much. If you can't totally remove the air conditioner sound, be SURE to get it as room tone!

Did I mention room tone? Yes? Okay, let's move on.

Cars, Traffic, Wind, Weather – Uncontrollable sounds of traffic passing may or may not ruin a scene. If the scene is outdoors on a city street, the sound of traffic is expected. However, you still don't want it on your dialog track if you can help it. (I'll explain why in a bit when I discuss DM&E's.) If you can work with the AD (assistant director) to time the take between passing cars, great! This will help.

Sometimes you still can't avoid it and will just have to make do to cut as much out as possible. Try using a wind muff. Also referred to as a "dead cat," fuzz ball, and many other things, these are the typically gray fuzzy mic coverings that you see on the end of a boom pole on professional productions in film and news gathering. While they are designed to cut wind noise from the mic (which they do superbly well), they can also partially cut down some unwanted ambient noises that sound like wind, such as a car passing or rain on a roof. It will not totally remove these sounds, but it can help to reduce them, and when combined with tweaking the recorder settings for low cut and gain, plus experimenting with mic direction again, you may be able to almost remove the sound of a passing car from being recorded even though everyone on set heard it.

When people on set begin looking at you like you're crazy or stupid because you say you didn't hear that car, squeak, thump, or air conditioner come on, don't fret. It just means you're getting good at cutting unwanted noises out of your recordings. Or it means you weren't paying attention and using critical listening skills. If it's the latter, you should worry. If it's the former, just smile and say "didn't come through my mic."

Actors – No, not what they say … what they do! Yes, if an actor isn't speaking for a moment and puts on a jacket, record that sound of the jacket being put on. However, if the actor is speaking *while* putting on a jacket, you have a problem. The jacket noise must be minimized. And if possible, get the AD to make the actor do the motion again, but without speaking, so you can record the action sound ("live Foley") for use in post. Here's why…

DM&E's

Dialog, Music, and Effects. Elements of the post-production process, these are the three groups of sub-mix that you must have, unique each to itself, in order to have your movie get distribution, especially overseas (the best place for micro-budget films to actually make a little money, usually). These sub-mixes, or "stems," seem simple on the surface as the dialog mix would contain all the dialog, the music mix has all the music, and the effects mix has all the sound effects. Right? Yes and no.

The dialog tracks must be able to be replaced for the foreign language versions of the film. So, if you have within your dialog track the sound of an actor putting on a jacket, you must also have that sound on your effects stem, without any dialog over it. NEVER let any dialog exist on the M or E stem – something for the post sound guy to know. Likewise, try not to have any action sounds in your dialog tracks, especially on TOP of the dialog where it's hard to remove. The movie must sound the same whether it's your actors speaking or Thai voice actors who read their lines in a booth.

In post, you check this by muting the dialog stem and listening to the scene to see if it still sounds the same, just with no sound coming out of the actors' mouths. If it doesn't, you have to make it sound the same, using Foley sounds or "canned" sound effects.

Help your post sound while you're still in production by thinking about DM&E's, preparing for them, and trying to not only separate as much noise from the actors' lines as possible, but capture separately on a "wild take" any sounds that you can't avoid being on top of the dialog. If possible, even have the actors run their lines wild, without moving through putting on a jacket. Then at least you have a clean take of the dialog. You can also have the actors run the scene action without speaking, for the FX track. Sometimes this works, sometimes not, and sometimes you don't have time to do it.

If all of this prep and thinking ahead goes wrong, or if problems can't be avoided, that's when you find yourself "looping" the actors, or recording ADR (automatic dialog replacement, which is *not* automatic). ADR is a pain in the butt, and costs money. Think ahead. A minute on set can save an hour in the post studio.

4 EXT. MIC PATTERNS - DAY

Let me repeat what I said in Scene 1: A shotgun microphone is NOT the end-all of movie mics! It will NOT work in every situation, and is NOT always the best thing to have hanging off the end of your boom. In fact, a shotgun mic should probably be used no more than about 25% of the times that they get used in indie films. Why, you ask?

> ME
> Would you use the same camera lens for every scene of every movie?

> CAMERA JOCKEY
> It depends on the movie and shot compositions.

> ME
> Indeed. So there may be a movie that could purposefully be designed to shoot with a single lens, like a 50mm, but in general, you're going to want a full array

of lenses in your bag, correct? Like an 18, 25, 35, 50, 85, and maybe a 100?

CAMERA JOCKEY
Yeah, exactly. You need to be able to change lenses depending on the situation to get the composition you want. And you have to consider the speed of the lens, and the ...

ME
Hold up there, camera dude. This book is about audio, so let's leave our lens description with primes, and forget about T-stops for now.

CAMERA JOCKEY
Okay, fine. Sheez.

Here it is:

Think of microphones like camera lenses. The recorder (Zoom H4n, Sound Devices 702, etc.) is like the camera body. One does the recording of the data, and has all the fancy settings; the other actually collects the data to be recorded.

Microphone = Lens
Field Recorder = Camera body

Let it sink in, and remember it. Now, let's explain why this is the case, and why it's important to understand.

Most common microphones fall into two basic

categories (with exceptions that are specialty mics you won't need for movies). Dynamic and Condenser. Dynamic mics are more for stage work, as they are less sensitive, and better at hiding little un-wanted noises the performer might make. Rarely are dynamics used in film, because we want to hear everything the actor does ... every part of the movement of his mouth, the little clicks and smacks in his teeth and cheeks. These things all fall into drawing the audience into suspension of disbelief, because when we are speaking with someone in person, we hear those tiny noises whether we realize it or not, and our brain processes them. So, in cinema, we need them to be there, too, so that it sounds real. If it sounds real, the audience will believe it, whether it looks real or not. Condenser mics capture all of these tiny nuances.

Within condensers there are large diaphragm and small diaphragm – the diaphragm being the "ear drum" element of the microphone that responds to sound waves in the air. Large diaphragm condensers are typically used in studio applications for musical vocals, voice-over, and acoustic instruments. There are some situations where they can be useful on a movie set, but those are fairly rare. The **small diaphragm condensers** are what we want. These look similar to what you're used to, being basically shaped like a shotgun mic (since a shotgun mic is a type of small diaphragm condenser), usually less than or about an inch in diameter and ranging in length from about four inches to a foot and a half or more.

Condenser microphones require power, whether by on-board battery or phantom power. I'll get to the power discussion later.

The most important thing you need to understand about any microphone is its pickup pattern. Realize that different mics have different patterns, and know how to use which one when.

CAMERA JOCKEY
Wait, what's a "pickup pattern?"

ME
Glad you asked.

Pickup patterns are the shape of the imaginary field (like a force field) surrounding the microphone in which the microphone can hear and collect sound. These patterns vary by type of microphone, and each has a different application. If you find yourself with a box full of mics, you'll be able to tell which one is what by pictograms that most manufacturers etch into the microphone body. I'll describe the pictograms as I walk through the pickup patterns.

Also, I'll associate the mic pattern to a lens length, for you camera-jockeys reading this. Remember though, because I list a lens length with a pickup pattern does not mean you should be using that mic if you are using that lens. My analogy there is to relate the width of image captured to the width of sound area that will be captured. As such, I'll list the patterns in order from widest to tightest, shortest to farthest.

The ranges, or distances, that I'll list are for the distance the microphone will be from the actors' mouths. If you have a group of actors with dialog, you'll need them all inside the radius listed, or you'll need to find another solution than the pattern listed - perhaps a different mic pattern, or adding a lavaliere mic or second boom.

Alternately, you could convince the director and the DP to shoot the scene differently so that you get a close shot on each individual actor for all of their lines. This is a boon to the sound department, but a pain in the ass for the DP, depending on the scene, so don't count on it to happen. Understand your equipment and know how to adapt.

The most common microphone pickup patterns include:

OMNI (omm-knee) -- Think 18mm lens.

Pictogram: a circle.

BEST USES:
- Interiors
- Exteriors
- Close range group dialog (<2ft)
- Hidden plant mic
- Lavaliere

This mic will hear everything around it in a spherical pattern, radiating from the pickup element at the end of the mic opposite the cable input.

Omni's can be very useful, especially as "plant" mics (hidden somewhere on set to pick up an intended sound), or in case there is a group of people sitting around a small table with dialog bouncing person to person.

Lavalieres are typically omni patterned because as the actor turns his head, the omni pattern of the lav doesn't care, and still picks up the audio smoothly and evenly.

Omni mics also typically have a very short range, so while they pick up every sound in every direction, they'll only hear things that are near to them, unless there's something very loud going on at a distance. So you won't have to worry about hearing the guy walking in the apartment upstairs, as long as you've set your recorder filters and gain correctly (we'll discuss that later).

Good examples of this pattern in a boom-mountable mic: Sennheiser ME-62, Audio Technica 4022 and 4049b, Neumann KM183, and the Rode NT55, which has changeable heads of both omni and cardioid. As usual, mics are available from brands such as Schoeps that are excellent, but more of a Hollywood budget. With my examples I will attempt to keep things reasonable, though not the cheapest you can find. Don't cheap out if you can afford a good mic.

CARDIOID (car-dee-oyd) -- Think 35mm lens.

Pictogram: a circle with a dimple at the bottom.

BEST USES:
- Interiors
- Exteriors
- Close range dialog (<4ft)
- When need to avoid close ambient noises like fluorescent lights or computer fans
- Excellent for a live room (heavy reverb)
- Hidden plant mic

One of the most useful and common mic patterns, the cardioid is an excellent all-around mic for close-range dialog in reasonably quiet environments. Every movie set should have at least one good cardioid condenser on hand! Whether indoors or out, a good cardioid can give you smooth clear dialog because of its directionality that only picks up sounds in front of it. There is no rear field reception (behind the mic, where the cable inserts). However, the cardioid does pick up sounds to its sides. Because of this, noises behind it that are loud enough to bounce off of walls might still be heard.

The cardioid does, however, have a relatively close range of reception, slightly farther than an omni, so careful balance of gain and filters can again give you clear dialog while deadening the environment. Cardioids excel in heavy reverb rooms by easing back the gain on the recorder, setting the low-cut (a.k.a. high-pass) filter correctly, and keeping a close mic placement - within 2 feet of the actor's mouth. See Chapter 12 for more details on this technique.

Some lavalieres use this pattern, but mic placement is critical with a lav of this type. You should generally avoid lavs that aren't omni.

Examples: Sennheiser ME-64, Audio Technica 4051b, Neumann KM184. Countless excellent cardioids are on the market. Be careful not to get one that is intended for instruments and not vocals, however.

HYPER-CARDIOID -- Think 50mm lens.

> **Pictogram:** bulbous, uneven figure-eight; a narrowed cardioid "apple" with a small loop where the leaves would be.

BEST USES:
- Interiors or Exteriors
- Close to Medium range group dialog (<6 to 8ft)
- Low-budget Boom-pole Champion
- Best solo or two-shot dialog pattern
- If you can only afford one mic, this is it!

Hyper-cardioid mics are perhaps the least known and simultaneously most useful mic pattern for film. They are tighter than cardioid and have little or no side field to the pickup. The area of reception is wide enough to not have to move during a close two shot, yet tight enough that lateral ambient sounds fall off nicely. The only drawback is the miniscule rear pickup field, but with mindful mic placement the rear field here is almost inconsequential.

They work exceptionally well for interiors, focusing tightly at close range and reducing ambient reverb almost as well as a cardioid. They are likewise great for exterior close and medium shots. Unfortunately they aren't tight enough to focus on dialog from a long distance, so you'll have to plan for this with the director if you're shooting with only one mic, which is likely, given the moderately high prices of hyper-cardioid mics.

Recommended good examples of this mic pattern exist in the Neumann KM-185, Audio Technica AT 4053b, and Oktava MK-012 (which can be used with interchangeable capsules to make it Omni, Cardioid, or Hyper-cardioid also).

Hang one of those off your boom and your sound will be transformed into a smooth, even, noise free (if you do the rest of your job right) moment of ecstasy for your dialog editor. As a bonus, these mics don't cost nearly as much as the "industry standard" mics by Schoeps and Sennheiser that you'll read about on the next page.

SUPER-CARDIOID *without interference tube*

-- Think 85mm lens. Perfect portraits.

Pictogram: two figure-eights, one long and one short, crossing each other to form a fat "t" that looks like a Flour De Lis.

BEST USES:

- Interiors
- Exteriors
- All dialog ranges short of 20 ft. or so
- Boom-pole Co-Champion, for larger budgets

Super-cardioid doesn't automatically mean shotgun, even if the terms have become synonymous for many people. How do you tell the difference? Is it labeled as super-cardioid, with the same pictogram as a shotgun, but it does NOT have the fish-gill slits running all the way down the side? Then it's a non-shotgun super-cardioid. There will be a few slits near the end, as the cardioid and hyper-cardioid have, but these mics will not be covered with perforations like the shotguns.

A non-shotgun super-cardioid could quickly become your favorite mic. The examples in production are superb, with immaculate sound and perfect tight targeting characteristics. They are just as versatile as the hyper-cardioid, except for having a slightly tighter reception area. If you ever listen through one, you will want one. The problem is affording one. These tend to be ludicrously expensive.

Examples: the Schoeps Collette Series (modular) MK41, Sennheiser MKH 50.

Yes, one of these mics could change your life as a film audio specialist. One could also bankrupt you if you aren't an income producing professional.

SUPER-CARDIOID *with interference tube*
-- Think 100mm+ lens.

This is the SHOTGUN microphone pattern! Read Carefully!

> **Pictogram:** two figure-eights, one long and one short, crossing each other to form a fat "t" that looks like a Flour De Lis.

BEST USES:
- Exteriors – (with exceptions) do not use indoors if other mics are available
- Medium to Long range dialog (>6 to 8ft or more)
- Can be used closer

I'll repeat: Shotgun microphones are not generally designed to be used indoors. Yes, they get used indoors all the time, even by the pros occasionally. I'm sure you've probably gotten what you deem as great audio from a shotgun used indoors. I'm sure it was fine, but not actually great. Shotguns won't capture great audio indoors, compared to hyper-cardioids, cardioids, or non-shotgun super-cardioids. There are exceptions to every rule, but in this case, to take advantage of the exceptions you really need to know more about how they work than you probably do now or than I will be explaining here. It's quite complex. A simplified version:

You see the slits that look like gills along the sides of

shotgun mics? Those are interference tube inlets. Basically, one reason shotguns are so target specific, or tightly directional – which is the reason everyone wants to use them *all the time*, thinking that will help cut down on picking up ambient noise – is because of their ability to receive sound from the sides of the mic and filter that from what it transmits down the cable. It removes a great deal of the lateral noise from the signal. Great! Yes, outdoors it is.

The problem indoors is that what you're trying to focus on, like the actor's voice, is also bouncing off the walls – from the sides – in a natural reverb. The shotgun mic doesn't know that you meant to hear what it's hearing from the sides, and it tries to filter it out. But it's also in the primary signal from the front. This causes a problem, resulting in reduced signal, hollow or unnatural sound, and sometimes a crackling or electronic static sound that I refer to as "shotgun sizzle." That sizzle can be very annoying to try and remove in post, and the hollow sound left behind always needs extra help to sound nice. So be nice to your post-production sound man – often on small productions that's also the picture editor, who is often also the director, who is often also the camera operator, which would mean that's you. Be nice to yourself, and get better quality sound for your production by using one of the mics that are intended for interiors when you're shooting interiors.

Now, how are shotguns useful? They are superb outdoors. Open areas where there are no (or few and far away) walls to collect and bounce back the sounds that you're trying to pick up in front are the natural playground for shotguns. And the super-cardioid pattern (or lobar, depending on what manufacturer is writing the spec sheet) is especially useful outdoors as well.

Shooting on a crowded city street? Fire up the shotgun and cut out the ambient sounds more than you'd even expect, if you do it right (see chapter 14). Shooting in the woods? No problem. Shooting a medium or long shot in a field and can't get close to the actors without getting in frame? Shotgun time. There are even different shotguns for different distances.

The longer the shotgun mic, the farther away it will hear things in a tight pattern. If you're trying to hear what someone is saying ten or twenty feet away, a medium length or possibly even a short shotgun is fine. These are typically about a foot or less in length. If you're trying to hear an actor who is more than about twenty feet away, use a long shotgun. These are typically sixteen inches or more, and always draw comments from the peanut gallery when they're removed from the case and mounted up.

There are too many to list all, and many are ludicrously expensive as well. But some good examples of industry standard shotguns on a budget include: Sennheiser ME-66 (medium) and ME-67 (long), Audio Technica BP4073 (mid) and BP4071 (long).

5 INT. MICROPHONE USES - DAY

Now that you're familiar with the most commonly used microphone types and pickup patterns, it's time to consider how mics are used during production. Different mics have different specific applications yet many will serve more than one purpose, as you've learned in chapter four. How do you know what's best for what situation? How do you plan the equipment for the shot?

> DIRECTOR
> This is a continuous medium with a short dolly in and pan. We have four actors, three sitting and one walking around the room. All have lines. I want to get it in one take.

> YOU (SOUND MIXER)
> Ummm... okay...

Nightmare! How do you catch all of that in one take? Well, if you've only got one mic, you can't, unless all four actors are within four feet of each other. You'll have to convince the director to either rent an additional mic or two, or shoot differently. However, for the sake of this chapter, let's consider that you have more than one mic. Where do you begin in setting up for this shot?

BOOM! Boom always comes first. Never roll a take without a boom swung just out of frame. For this hypothetical shot, you would want either a hyper-cardioid or a cardioid on the end of the boom. Either of those patterns will allow you to swing boom between actors as they speak and give you some leeway if you aren't quite on target yet when the line begins. They also will allow you to stay planted between two actors if they are having a rapid-fire exchange and not have to try to keep up with whose line is next. Let's not forget to also always use at least a foam windscreen, even indoors, when recording dialog.

So, consider that you have a hyper-cardioid mounted on a boom and are ready for the shot in question. No? Oh yes, other mic options…

On a Stand! It may seem obvious to some who have music or stage backgrounds, but often a mic stand is hard to find on a movie set. It shouldn't be. For our shot here, I would likely want to place a cardioid on a stand, gain cranked, aiming in from the side least conspicuous to the camera and lighting. This would be a good backup in case I missed something with the boom.

I've also used mic stands for special tricks when working alone. One example, while on a time limited shoot and not wanting to have time consumed in post for sound effects, I used a mic stand with its pivot head loosened and a cardioid on a boom arm (a pole about 3 feet long that mounts atop a stand) to capture the sounds of feet scrambling on the pavement during a fight scene. I had the boom for dialog, the stand for action, recorded on separate tracks. Post took two minutes for the scene instead of two hours of creating Foley fight and foot noises (although punches were added).

Stands are useful. Always have one with you, especially one with a short boom arm.

Plant it! The tricks above about using a stand technically fall under the category of plant mics. Think of a plant mic as, well, a potted plant in the scene that can hear. You "plant" a mic by hiding it somewhere in the scene, close to what you want to hear, but out of sight of the camera and out of the way of the actors. Using plant mics is a valuable technique that pays for the little extra effort it requires many times over. Some examples:

I once taped a cardioid to a table leg in order to have a backup to the boom mic that I wasn't sure was going to cut it in the situation we found ourselves. I was right. The cardioid sounded much cleaner and with much less reverb than the shotgun on the boom. I know, I said don't use a shotgun indoors. I'll elaborate on this particular situation in Chapter 16 – Know When to Say No. It was a hard lesson learned which you can benefit from.

In another instance, I planted a mic on a short stand between an actor's legs as he sat playing guitar. The shot was from behind him, so the mic was out of sight. Yet the hidden Neumann mic perfectly captured the live guitar as he played (his left hand was in shot) and it was actually that track that became the music in one version of the trailer for the film. Did we need it for his dialog? No. Did we use it later and get major praise for it? Yep.

Plant mics are also useful when an actor turns away from the others while delivering dialog. In our hypothetical here, the one actor moving around could turn her back to the boom and keep speaking, while the boom must remain on the other three actors who are also speaking. Plant a mic that will be in her face when she turns around. It won't hear much of what else is said but it will catch what you otherwise would miss and have to loop or catch wild.

Lavalieres! Whether wired or wireless, body mounted lavaliere (lav) mics can be extremely useful. They can also be an absolute nightmare that will make you wish wireless electronics didn't exist. I prefer to avoid using lavs if at all possible, although they do have their place in the kit.

Why do I not like them? They're frustrating to hide and avoid clothing dragging across them for a nice "ccccrrrrraaaccckle" sound in the middle of a take, for one. Hiding lavs effectively while maintaining their audio integrity is an art unto itself. If you're good at it, you can find work, especially in television. But it's a huge pain.

Another aspect of lavs: Hiding thin mics and transmitter packs under clothing and even inside undergarments is not uncommon in film. Keeping professional composure while hiding a wire inside a brassiere that's being worn by a gorgeous actress is, well, required. Maintain professional composure with your mind on the job, or baseball. And yes, the same applies when genders are reversed.

I prefer to avoid using lavs, because in the end, while they can sound good, they just don't sound as nice as a "real" mic that's properly tuned and placed near an actor's mouth. Sometimes, however, they are necessary – such as in our hypothetical scene.

One way to avoid missing any dialog would be to wire the moving actor with a wireless lav. However, some factors to consider before resorting to this:

- No lav will match tone with the boom mic exactly. Some lavaliere mics actually suck quite badly. If you're going to have one, be sure it's good quality. Here I'm speaking of the microphone element itself, not the transmitter or receiver.

- Cheap wireless sets (the transmitter and receiver) often suffer from a maddening problem that's sometimes referred to as "fades." This is where the sound dips away, with a swooshing sound replacing it, as radio interference or blocked or weak signals come into play. Wireless units able to avoid this problem tend to be painfully expensive and prohibitive of the micro-budget crew to own. If you aren't spending over $1,200 on a single body pack/receiver set, you're might get a unit that will frustrate you, although some in the $600 range aren't awful. Wired lavs obviously won't suffer this issue, but then you have to hide the wire – across the set, not just on the body – and your actor must be stationary. In that case, why have a lav instead of a good boom mic? Interviews in documentaries are about the extent of use for wired lavs, in my opinion.

- Clothing can interfere not only by scratching against the mic, but also by creating static, which causes fades. If your actors are wearing wool, look out. I felt especially guilty once when I had to tape a body pack transmitter to an actor's bare back (under his shirt) because his wool suit pants were killing my signal.

So, using the appropriate mics in the various ways mentioned, we can get full coverage audio for the scene without missing any dialog. These few mic usages – boom, stand, plant, and lavaliere – will get you through all possible production sound scenarios. If they don't, you're looking at an ADR (dialog replacement) session in your future. Dragging actors to a sound booth can be as much of a challenge as getting them to match vocal performances.

6 EXT. THE RECORDER - NIGHT

For non-sound people, the portable digital field recorder seems to present an intellectual mystery akin to Pandora's box or quantum mechanics. However, they really aren't that complex to master – no worse than a professional grade camera – if you know what the various settings mean and understand how they will affect your recordings.

Allow me to open the mystery box and explain its contents, one piece at a time, looking first at which recorder settings you need to learn how to adjust, to what, and why.

FILE FORMATS

Your Mp3 player sounds pretty good, right? And those files take up way less space than .WAV files, so why not record in Mp3? Being too tech laden to bother explaining here, let me just say this: Don't record audio for your film in Mp3 format. It is a compressed file, and even at its highest quality settings an Mp3 cannot match the clarity and aural spectrum of a WAV file. For a short film, it is fine for your music track to originate as a 320 kHz Mp3, but even then, don't trust your dialog tracks to it.

A WAV file has the advantage of clarity, depth and detail when it comes to standard recorder file formats. Almost all recorders offer WAV format as an option. If yours doesn't, get a new one. The bit and sample rate discussion below relates to numbers associated with WAV files.

What happens when you set your recorder to WAV and stereo? Your recording is a single file, in stereo form (a left channel and right channel), even if you have only one mic. If you have two mics recording simultaneously, you will likely be recording one mic to the left side and one mic to the right side of the single audio file. Or, if you have "mono-mix" turned on, you're recording an instant mix of the two mics, replicated onto the left and right channels of the single file. Now the two separate signals from the two separate mics are permanently mixed at a set level. You don't want this, if you can help it. While you can separate the left and right in post software, it remains much easier to just record in BWF if you can. This is why BWF exists. A .**BWF**, or **Broadcast WAV File**, is simply a wrapper package for recording separate signals into their own separate WAV files, but packaged together, in sync as they were recorded.

So, **a BWF file is a grouping of multiple WAV files**. Let's say you record with two mics, to two separate tracks in your recorder. In this instance, when you set your recorder to BWF, you are actually recording two WAV files, one for each mic, that are being wrapped up together into a single file, or BWF. Typical media players cannot decipher a BWF and often when a producer downloads your data from the recorder onto his laptop he will instantly scream because "there is no sound coming from any of these recordings!" Don't panic. Import the BWFs into a Digital Audio Workstation (DAW – professional audio software, such as Pro Tools, Cubase, Logic, Sonar, etc.) and the DAW will decipher the BWF file and show you each track that was recorded as a separate WAV file. It doesn't matter if you've recorded a single track with one mic, or six tracks with six mics, there will be a single BWF file, and within it a separate WAV file for each track recorded. This is how you want your audio recorded for your film.

Keeping the audio from each microphone as discrete (separated) as possible, recording each onto its own track in the recorder, allows your post audio mixer and dialog editor to do their jobs much more effectively. It allows them to cut and blend and add processors, EQ, and so forth to each source separately, making it all sound more cohesive and smooth. It is much harder to achieve a smooth mix live on set than it is in post. Allow the post editor to do it, and record each mic at its own optimal level, onto its own track, within a BWF file. Record in BWF and all your WAVs will be groovy.

THE BITS and SAMPLES

Bit Depth and Sample Rate are perhaps two of the most misunderstood yet fundamental aspects of audio recording knowledge. Without getting too elaborate...

First, what they aren't. The "bits" of your

recording have nothing to do with your computer operating system. The bit depth of your recording is only concerned with itself and could care less that you have a 64 bit operating system. Forget that mental association.

Likewise, the sample rate, denoted by kilohertz, or frequency, has nothing to do with the audible frequencies that we hear. Human hearing ranges from roughly 20 Hz to 20 kHz. The sample rate of your recording has nothing to do with this spectrum, at least not directly. They are two totally separate measurements. Forget that mental association as well.

So, what are these mysterious numbers?

Bit Depth represents the clarity of your recording. The higher the number is set for the bit depth, the more range of volume you can adjust when mixing and still avoid hearing things that don't belong in your recording – but were there anyway – like hisses and hums from poor power sources, not so great cables, or so-so microphone pre-amps.

Music CDs are output in 16 bit depth. Many movies have been done in 16 bit, and still are. However, to help ensure you achieve the best possible sound, especially when dealing with a recorder that's likely not a $10,000 Zaxcom or equivalent, you should always set your bit depth at 24. This will help you achieve clearer sound by giving your post production mixer more range within which to work.

Sample Rate relates to the detail you are capturing in your recording. It basically is how many times the recorder's processor has taken a "sample" of the audio signal and layered it onto itself to create the data that is the recording. The higher the sample rate, or number of digital samples taken, the more realistic and natural your recording will sound. With low sample rates, you may still hear a person speaking clearly (Clarity is part of bit depth, remember?), but it may sound a little muffled or otherwise lacking and you can't quite put your finger on why. Turn the sample rate up and try it again. You'll discover what's missing: the higher audible frequencies.

The high frequencies are not only important for things like cymbals and glasses clinking together, but even for recording the deepest (low frequency) male voices. In fact, the high frequencies that become more apparent and detailed as sample rate climbs are perhaps more important when recording low voices. Confused?

Remember what I said about needing to hear all of the little clicks and pops that our mouths make when we speak in order for it to sound real? Well, many of those sounds reside in the higher audible frequency ranges. So if you're not recording those ranges sufficiently when an actor is speaking – especially an actor with a deep voice – he will sound muffled, flat, and synthetic.

Now, to be clear, a low sample rate that will begin losing that detail for the average listener is somewhere below a 30 kHz sample. Music CDs, which are inferior to DVD or Blue-ray audio, are 44.1 kHz. DVD audio is typically 48 kHz, as is Blue-ray, although Blue-ray is capable of using a 96 kHz sample rate for even greater detail in the higher ranges, which high-end home theater sound systems sometimes can reproduce. So what's best? What to use? If higher is better you should use 96 or even 192 if available, right? No, not really.

192 kHz is only useful for super clear classical music being listened to by the most anal-retentive audiophile on speakers that cost more than a compact car. 96 kHz is the maximum to bother with when recording for film. However, this has some drawbacks as well.

Raising the numbers for both bit depth and sample rate have two effects overall: your recording is clearer and more detailed, and your memory card fills up *very* quickly. High sample rates make your file sizes huge. The more "samples" in a recording, the more data. The more data, the larger the file size. This can also become a problem when importing your recordings into your computer and DAW. I have seen even the heartiest computers freeze when presented with too much of a good thing.

Stay with 48 kHz sample rate and you will be fine. It's all a DVD can use anyway, and better than you'll hear on any streaming service.

Now here's one part that can get unnecessarily complex and confusing in almost every book on sound for film that I've ever read.

Frame Rate. In this world of all digital that we now live in, frame rate is almost obsolete unless you're on a project that's using actual film cameras. But this book is designed for micro budget, and I'm going on the notion that 99.9% of micro budget films and docs are now shot on digital. That means that frame rate doesn't matter a hill of beans for the sound man. But just to make everyone happy, you should go ahead and set the frame rate in your recorder, if it even has an option to do so (many cheaper ones don't anymore).

Ask the cinematographer what frame rate he or she is shooting, and be specific. If he says, "24," ask if it's true 24 or 23.97. You will need to know exactly. Then, set your digital recorder to whatever frame rate he says by finding it in the menus of the audio recorder. That's it. Done. If you're both shooting digital, without any actual reels turning to vary the speed of things, there's nothing else to worry about. The digital audio files get so chopped up in post and slid all over the timeline that sync is no longer a complex problem for the production sound mixer. Asymmetrical speed calculations and pull down rates don't have to be worried over.

The other sync item that comes up is **Time Code.** Time code isn't as difficult to deal with as you would think. If you're on a shoot where someone is demanding TC be used, first try to talk them out of it. If they persist, tell them to set it up. I'm not getting into time code in this text because there are too many variations of how to set things up, and frankly, with digital cinema cameras and digital audio recorders, it's not necessary anymore.

NOOB
But how do we sync picture to sound in post-production then?

Simple. The slate. Clacker. Sticks. Whatever you call them, or if you don't have any and use your hands to actually clap loudly, that sharp peak that's created in the waveform of the audio on both the audio recorder and the camera's audio is how you sync. Line them up in the NLE (non-linear-editor…video editing software) when the picture edit is done and audio files are dropped in. Then the dialog editor can make minute adjustments as needed. Of course you do need a slate board to write the scene name or number and take number on, which should be called out for the mic to hear just prior to the sticks dropping. Standard procedure. You probably already know about that if you're a camera operator or director. If you're a noob PA who's been handed this book because you're running sound tomorrow, you're welcome, and read faster.

OTHER SETTINGS

Low Cut/High Pass Filters are going to become your best friend as a location sound mixer. Pay attention here. These are named such because of the frequency ranges of sound that they affect.

A simple explanation of frequency: A high note in music is a high frequency; a low musical note is a low frequency.

A "low cut" filter cuts off the low frequency sounds below (or lower than) whatever frequency you set for the filter. A "high pass" filter allows sounds above the point you set the filter to pass through unaffected. So yes, "low cut" and "high pass" are two ways of saying the same thing. [Conversely, low pass/high cut filters are the opposite of what I just described. We don't deal with those in location sound, however.]

Now, don't be alarmed. These filters don't actually eliminate all sounds below your set frequency.

They typically step down the gain input of frequencies in a stair-step pattern.

Let's say you set your recorder's low cut filter to 100 Hz. That's very near the normal lowest frequencies that a typical male voice will make, so you're not losing any dialog detail. But by setting the filter to "on" and at that frequency, the recorder will turn down the gain - typically by 6 or 12 decibels of volume, or dB - for each 15 Hz step down in frequency. Again, this is typical. Some recorders allow both the distance stepped down and the dB pad per step to be set by the user. Most cheaper recorders do not allow this variable, and simply give you options of what frequency to begin the stair steps, if they offer any filter options beyond "on" or "off."

Why do you need to use the low cut filter? Noise. Lowering the recorded volume of lower notes, or frequencies in relation to the higher frequencies where our vocal dialog resides (about 100hz to 4kHz for the highest pitched female screams), we can eliminate much of the ambient (or environmental, or background noise) in our recordings. Not only does activating the low cut filter significantly quiet things like air conditioners and car engines in the background, but it will also eliminate much of a room's ambient hum, which I refer to as "room boom."

Room boom is sometimes used to refer to a room's natural reverberation as well (boominess of noises because of reverb or echo). However, it is this natural reverberation that can make a room loud without any sound being made in it. It just sort of hums. It's quiet, and we usually don't notice it with our ears, but it's there, and is much more noticeable in recordings made with the super sensitive condenser microphones that we use when making movies. By eliminating this room boom hum, we create much cleaner dialog tracks that are easier to work with in post-production and make the director happier to listen back to the take during production. It will sound clearer, cleaner, and the actors' voices will stand out with a fuller, less muddy sound.

There are circumstances where you might want to specifically capture very low pitched sounds. Recording dialog is not one of those circumstances. If scene has dialog, turn the low cut filter on. Normal default settings on most recorders are usually 80 Hz, to avoid cutting any fullness of sound from a deep voice of a male actor. If you're having trouble with ambient hum type noise, though, try turning the low cut up to 100, 120, or even as high as about 160hz to clean up the recording. Be aware, however, that anything above about 120 Hz and you will begin noticing a slight tininess, or thinness, to some deeper voices. Balance is the key. You'll have to use your judgment and ears to decide which way sounds best and if the compromise is worth it.

Limiters can be useful at times. These limit the input volume to a certain maximum, to eliminate clipping of the recording. Clipping occurs when a noise is sudden and sharp, or when you just have the gain set too high. If your gain is set correctly and you are having clipping (or peaking), you might try turning on the recorder's limiter. It can soften these peaks and make things sound normal. Sometimes. The problem is that most of the cheaper field recorders also have cheaper limiters in their circuitry and have no adjustments available. Often times these limiters are too "soft" and produce a bouncing effect to the sound, squashing the volume of sounds adjacent to the peak, along with the peak. It comes out sounding bad and unusable.

If you're peaking hard and there's no dialog immediately adjacent the peak, you could turn the limiter on and solve the problem. But if the peak occurs during dialog, the limiter will cripple your dialog track by giving it an inconsistent volume. In that situation it's best to leave the limiter off and deal with the peak in post where it can be massaged out with software or simply muted. If the peak is coming as part of the dialog (yelling, screaming, etc.), then you may need to turn down the gain or take more drastic measures, which I will discuss in a later chapter.

To sum up limiters: Don't trust them to always fix clipping or peaks. I prefer recording with limiters off unless absolutely necessary. It's easier to fix a peak in post than it is to fix a dead spot in your dialog.

Automatic Gain vs. Manual Control. Use your ears and manual gain control. Auto gain can at times be useful but you will never get a feel for adjusting the levels properly if you don't do it yourself. Play around with it. See how far the meters move under normal talking, loud talking, whispering, etc. Know the range your scene will have dynamically and adjust accordingly. Auto gain is about as useful as a bad limiter. Plus, if it messes up and you don't know it, you're screwed in post. Leave it off.

CONNECTIONS and ON-BOARD MICS

Your portable digital field recorder should have at the very least two balanced XLR type microphone inputs and be capable of providing phantom power to the external mics. TRS is another acceptable balanced microphone input, though I rarely have used them. Mic cables are usually XLR (the 3-pin type connectors). Being balanced, electronic hum within the device is eliminated, at least from that potential source. If a hum is heard, some recorders or interfaces have a "ground lift" feature that can take care of it. The input must be from a balanced source, such as XLR or TRS, in order for this to work, however.

Never use on-board (built-in to the recorder) microphones if you have a real condenser microphone available. Period. There should be enough XLR inputs on your recorder for all the mics you will use simultaneously. If not, buy a bigger recorder or get a mixer, which can take several mic inputs and output them into a single channel or stereo pair (or many more, depending on the mixer). You can feed the mix into the recorder's inputs via XLR. However, unless you are quite experienced with live sound mixing and recording mixing, I do not suggest this option. Get a larger recorder that can handle all the inputs at once onto separate tracks within the BWF.

RECORDING MEDIA

Recording media is typically the same as with cameras: Solid state data cards, such as SD or CF

(Compact Flash). Cards are especially nice and handy as they can be had cheaply, allowing you to save the original files without dumping them to a computer and overwriting the card with new ones. It's best to save the original media; at least until post production is complete, even if you have downloaded it to a computer or two. (Always back-up your files!) No special speed of cards are needed for audio, although I do recommend that if you are going to record with a 96kHz sample rate that you use a class 10 SD card to keep things operating smoothly.

An alternative to the cards that's more expensive and typically only found on high end or older recorders is HDD (Hard Disk Drive). This can be cumbersome for a few reasons: limited space, not usually easy to swap out, much more expensive per data capacity than SD cards, and they can make noise within the machine and cause interference in your recording (not typical).

Some recorders also use DVD-RAM or some other optical disc drive to record, or often instantly mirror and backup the HDD during recording. This is highly cumbersome and time consuming on set when swapping discs.

Yet another way, and what will eventually be the way to go once prices come down more, is to use SSD, or Solid State Drives. These are basically like highly concentrated, huge capacity SD cards all crammed together into one device. There are no moving parts, with nothing to make noise or break, so they carry all the benefit of card media except for size (SSD are smaller than HDD but much bigger than an SD card) and price. Currently, SSD are prohibitively expensive for most micro-budget sound recordists, and even if they weren't, the recorders that use them typically are (often $4,000 or more).

7 EXT. HEADPHONES - NIGHT

One of the most neglected, misunderstood pieces of a film sound kit is the headphones. Many people assume that headphones are headphones and whatever will do. This is far from the case. A good set of headphones can make your work on set better, as much as a bad or inadequate set can make your recording suck badly. So how do you know what to get? Which "cans" are best?

TYPES of HEADPHONES

There are four basic designs of **traditional headphones**:

- Open Back
- Closed Back
- On-ear (supra-aural)
- Over-ear (circum-aural)

These can be had in a full matrix of

configurations. The normal casual-music-listening headphones tend to be open back, on-ear design. Often having soft foam pads and barely squeezing head straps, these can be very comfortable to wear. However, they are not what you'll want to use for recording on set.

The **open back** design allows ambient sounds in. This is a great feature for joggers, so they don't get run over by cars. It's awful for a film sound recordist because it allows sounds that your microphone isn't hearing to get to your ears. These make it difficult to tell what you're recording versus what sounds are being filtered out of the mix by your expert selection of the proper microphone and recorder settings.

Closed back, over-ear (circum-aural) designs are what you want as the location sound recordist. These will block out ambient sound rather well, effectively sealing off your ears to the majority of sounds that aren't coming through your microphone. In addition, the over-ear design, which surrounds your ears instead of sitting on top of them, pressing the cartilage into the sides of your head – allows for better all day comfort. The springs that hold the ear cups ("cans") to your head already squeeze hard enough to drive you batty after six to eight hours, much less the all too common 12-14 hour days we find ourselves on set in indie-film. Comfort helps.

In-the-ear designs of headphones are becoming ever more popular with some people. These are not "ear-buds" like the ones that came with your iPod. These are in-ear monitors, similar to what stage musicians and singers often use. These can be exceptional at sealing off the ear canal from any sounds not coming from the microphone, depending on their design. Personally, I find these annoying after a while and prefer my old-school cans, despite the fact they can get sweaty and uncomfortable after extended use as well.

Regardless of whether you choose closed-back, circum-aural headphones or in-ear monitors, you should still remember to rest your ears whenever you get the opportunity. Fatigue can not only make a long day feel like a week, but ear fatigue can result in you missing sounds that you should be alert to while recording dialog, such as a cough in another room, or a distant train passing.

SPECIFICATIONS and FEATURES

When shopping for a good pair of headphones to use in film sound work, begin by shopping in the **studio monitor** section of the catalogs. Normal headphones are designed to make music sound good by upping the bass response or peaking the highs. Studio cans are designed to let the user hear exactly what the sound is, without any fluff. They give a flat "curve" frequency response, if you look at a graph. No one tonal range of sound is reproduced any louder than others.

These studio type headphones will have not only a more natural and accurate sound, but will cover the entire range of normal human hearing: from 20Hz to 20 kHz. Actually, most people's hearing goes away above 17 kHz-19 kHz. Still, your headphones should have a "frequency response" range that covers the full 20-20k. This will insure that you don't miss anything.

In addition to the natural, full sound and full

spectrum of hearing range that studio monitor headphones give you, another advantage is durability and comfort. Studio phones are usually made for professionals to use on a daily basis, for hours at a time. This means they're designed to hold up to that daily use and abuse, and are typically much more durable than music headphones. They're also typically designed to be more comfortable.

On a personal note, I feel I should mention the cable. With a straight cable, which I purchased for actual in-studio use, I have gotten tangled up in myself on set. Many, many times. It's maddening. For your own sanity and a more enjoyable experience with headphones in the field, go with a coiled cable set.

Studio headphones can range from about $50 to well over $400. However, there are several good sets available that will serve you well for years in the meat-and-potatoes $75-150 range. Look to models from Audio Technica, Sony, and Sennheiser to find excellent options for budget cans. Going upscale a bit you will find models from all of these and Beyerdynamic that have replaceable ear pads for when yours wear out. Which they will, eventually. My personal favorite headphones? The Audio Technica ATH-M50. They're pretty much perfect.

Once you find your set of headphones, always use them. Even when you work on a set where they provide equipment, bring your own cans. After a while you'll get used to how your headphones sound, and how certain sounds are heard in them. You'll know what's significant or not, and what will or won't be heard in the mix. Consistent usage of the same set of headphones is critical for the location recordist. It helps you become better at what you do.

8 INT. ASSEMBLE THE KIT - NIGHT

When considering the components of your kit and where to spend your money – or at least the majority of it – you must be realistic. Are you typically a one-man-show, running camera, lights, and audio all by yourself for small documentary type work, or are you a component of a team of people and your job is sound?

If you're currently a one person operation, don't buy gear that can only be used by someone who doesn't also have his or her hands on the camera. You can buy gear in phases. Get parts that will work for either scenario but be sure you get what will work for you now – not in some ideal dream world that may or may not exist in the near future.

SINGLE vs. DUAL SYSTEM RECORDING

If you are a one person crew, you will be faced with a decision that plagues many: record into the camera or on a separate recorder?

If you can at all afford a decent field recorder after buying your camera system, it is always best to record to a separate recorder. Use your camera audio (assuming it has audio capabilities) as a "scratch track," or a backup track of audio recorded in the camera, in sync with the picture.

Consider if you record only into your camera. You are limited to the audio settings contained in your camera's functions. Granted, some pro grade cameras have quite sophisticated audio capabilities. Most do not. Especially when considering the common DSLR's that most micro-budget film crews use now, you are drastically restricting your ability to capture good audio by using your camera as a primary audio recorder.

What if an audio field recorder had a little video camera built into it? Would you think that camera would be of the quality needed to shoot your feature film on? No? Then why would you want to use your camera to record your audio?

It's not really that cut and dried. However, what if your camera audio malfunctioned? Now what? Or, what if your camera settings don't allow you to adjust the low cut filter in the audio? What if you need more than one input, such as for a boom mic and a lavaliere? Or the real question: What if you want to get Hollywood film quality sound for your no budget indie film?

In all of these situations the answer is to run dual system audio, or record your audio to two locations: camera, and field recorder. Use the camera audio, in whatever form, as your scratch track to sync sound to picture and have your primary sound running on a dedicated and purpose built film audio recorder with a proper boom microphone positioned appropriate distance to the actors' mouths. This is the only way your sound will approach the big leagues. Be sure to clack sticks or have someone clap hands at the start of every take, whether you slate or not. The spike in the visible waveform in both recordings can be used in editing software to quickly and easily sync the two audio sources, without need for time code.

Even if you are a one person operation, you can still pull this off. Use a mic stand with a boom if you're conducting interviews. Or if you're run and gunning it, use a high quality camera mounted mic, but still record to a separate field recorder. Optimally, however, you need to find a sound recordist to run with you.

MOUNTING THE MICROPHONE and NOISE SUPPRESSION

Some microphones, such as the Rode Video Mic, are made for mounting camera-top on your DSLR's hot shoe and plugging in directly to your camera's 1/8" audio input. While this method works okay in some applications, I don't generally recommend it unless, as described above, you simply cannot have a sound recordist and you are working alone in a run and gun mobile situation. While there's nothing wrong with that mic and those like it, you simply cannot get cinematic sound without your mic closer to your subjects. Therefore, you should be mounting your small-diaphragm condenser dialog mic on a boom pole, or at very least a mic stand and positioning it appropriately to your subject.

Most of these mics come with a standard mic clip.

These are mostly useless unless you are mounting it on a fixed position stand or your sound guy has super soft hands and pays attention to his movements. When operating a boompole, it is critical to keep your hands still, even when using a shock mount. When using a clip mount, almost any subtle movement at all will be transmitted into the microphone and recorded. I've heard many good dialog takes be ruined by the sound man raising a finger or sliding his hand an inch down the pole. It can be awful, especially if you have an intern holding a boompole who doesn't care what's being recorded and doesn't bother listening to what he's recording.

Use a shock mount if at all possible. While some mics come with their own, this is not the norm and you will have to buy a separate one. A shock mount is a device that holds your microphone solidly while retaining it away from solid surfaces of the boompole or mic stand. These typically use a heavy rubber-band suspension, or some other shock absorbing design that prevents those tiny hand movements (or footsteps on hardwood, if you're using a stand) from reaching the mic as easily.

Another way unwanted noise enters the mic is via wind. This can be reduced some by using the little foam slip-on wind screens that are often included with the microphone, but if you're outdoors in any wind more than a breath, these will be highly insufficient.

If you can afford it, I recommend purchasing a blimp system. It will benefit your sound in countless ways, including providing you with a multi-point suspension shock mount that can easily be mounted to a boompole, and noise reduction that is typically much better than you will get from a simple foam windscreen. Usually a thread adapter is required to attach these to a mic stand but they mount directly to boompole threads.

A blimp system (the oblong, often gray, cylinders that are typically on the end of a professional's boompole when shooting outdoors) will let you use the shock mount without the blimp covering when you are indoors. Whether indoors or out, however, the blimp itself provides a certain level of attenuation (deadening of sound) which will help to eliminate wind noise, car noise, air conditioning noise, etc. etc. etc. The blimp also provides a place to better mount your fuzzy muff wind blocker. The combination of these elements: shock mount, blimp to protect the mic and shield some noise, and fuzzy wind blocker cover, combine to help smooth your sound. You will be amazed how much difference you actually hear. A decent blimp system is an excellent investment that I recommend to anyone serious about good film sound.

THIS POLE IS JUST RIGHT

There are a few things to consider when selecting a boompole. The limitations of trade-off here often cause professional sound guys to own more than one pole:

- Length – Will it collapse small enough for easy transport and recording in small spaces like bathrooms and closets? Will it extend far enough to reach in close overhead during a medium shot where you might be 12-15 feet or more from the actors?

- Weight – Is it lightweight enough to not kill your shoulders when held overhead for long stretches of time? When considering differences of ounces, with an average weight around 2 pounds, this may not seem like much. But small amounts of weight add up and stress over time. Lighter is better. Sometimes it's beneficial to have an ultra-light 6-9 foot pole in your kit in addition to the big 12-15 foot one.

Aluminum is cheaper and doesn't really weigh much more, but carbon fiber or graphite poles can feel better in the hand, even though they cost phenomenally more. It will depend on how cheap you are, and if you have any money left after buying a good mic – which should always come as first priority – as to whether you can justify the cost of a carbon pole.

Another big consideration is getting a pole with "cable through" already installed. I have worked with both cabled poles and those that I must gaff tape the cable to the pole to keep it from flopping around. Cable-through is so much better I can't describe it well enough. Just go with that if you can afford it. Also, get one with a side "exit" or XLR socket to attach your cable to the recorder. This will allow you to rest the end of the pole on your foot between takes without destroying your cable or connectors.

THE DEVIL in the DETAILS

Do not underestimate the value in having good quality mic cables, with good quality connectors. No matter how good your microphone and field recorder, if your cables suck you will have crappy sound. Why?

Imagine having a perfectly clear, full dialog take ruined by intermittent crackles and cut outs caused by loose or poorly soldered connectors wiggling in their sockets when you swing your boom from one actor to another. This happens. And it's a horrible way to die as a sound recordist, because the director will certainly kill you if you don't off yourself after hearing it on playback.

Pony up and spend the extra money to buy the best quality cables you can afford. You will thank yourself later.

Also where cables are concerned, remember to watch how you arrange them when hooking up your kit. Don't put stress on the connectors, and properly wrap and secure your extra cable length using the standard cable wrapping method. (Many videos exist online to show how this is done if you don't know what I'm talking about here. It's not something easily explained in writing.) Invest in some cheap Velcro cable management ties, too. Wild wires on set can become both maddening and dangerous if you get yourself tangled up in them. Nothing is more embarrassing than tripping over your own XLR cable. Trust me.

WHAT DO I DO WITH THIS BRICK?

Is your field recorder small and lightweight, or big and bulky? For the hand-held variety of recorders such as the H4n, I have variably either held it in one hand, wedged it against the boom, dropped it in a jacket pocket, or mounted it on a stand. That is, until

I discovered that the handlebar mount for my action-cam not only would mount to the ¼-20 threads of my recorder, but fit perfectly to my boompole, as though it were a handlebar. This discovery was a revelation that changed my on-set experience dramatically from frustratedly grabbing up and wrestling all my components for every setup, to simply putting on my headphones, picking up my stick, and turning everything on. If you work with a single mic and small recorder, it's a setup you will celebrate every time you're on set.

Alternately as I mentioned, I have also mounted the small recorders on mic stands, just to get them out of my hands. This works if you are able to be in a fairly static position with the boom. If you have to walk around to follow the actors, don't even bother with the on-stand method.

If your recorder is larger, such as a Sound Devices unit, get a decent quality carry bag and try not to put all of the stress from its weight on your neck. The harness systems you see the pros using that divert the weight to the shoulders are definitely worth the money if you're booming 8-12 hours a day.

So now you have your boompole, recorder, cables, mic, suspension and noise suppression system, and headphones. You are ready to rock out, right? Almost. Now you're ready to learn to use them successfully.

9 INT. POWER - DAY

DIRECTOR
Ok, back to position one. Let's try another one. Roll sound...

YOU (SOUND MIXER)
Sound has ... wait. Dead battery. I have to change batteries.

DIRECTOR
Waiting on sound!

BATTERIES, BATTERIES, BATTERIES!

Don't let this happen to you. It will anyway, but try to minimize it. Camera and electrical always blames sound for on-set delays. Most of the time it's not true. However, sometimes it is. Most of those times it could be avoided by not trusting batteries and preparing for them to die randomly and quickly.

One example: I once had to wire up six actors with wireless lavs for a scene. I had checked the batteries when they were last used a few hours earlier. However, the time taken to wire everyone up, and leaving them on as I finished each actor, meant that as soon as everyone else was ready to roll, my wireless units started dropping out with dead batteries. I had to scramble and change all of them while everyone began the cliché complaining of waiting on sound, even though I had been ready and waiting on lighting to be set for almost thirty minutes before my batteries all died at once.

This is simply a lesson to consider as far as having enough extra batteries for all of your gear if you are using alkaline, or to have extras for all of your gear on charge continuously if you're using rechargeables.

Another aspect to consider for battery life is phantom power. If your mic can accept a battery and run off of its own power, that typically will allow your recorder power to last much longer than if it is supplying phantom power to your microphone. All condenser mics require power to operate. Some can provide their own power, however. But only some of those actually sound decent when providing their own power, so that's another consideration that will require experimentation.

When using Sennheiser ME series mics with the K6 power units (a very common mic for low budget operations), I highly recommend using their battery. It will make a small recorder battery go from lasting about an hour to four or six hours. If you're running a Sound Devices or similar unit with a heavy duty rechargeable battery and a nice-sounding built-in mic pre-amp though, it's well worth it to allow the recorder to provide phantom power to the mic. It will still last quite a while.

To repeat my earlier statement: If you're currently a one person operation, don't buy gear that can only be used by someone who doesn't also have his or her hands on the camera. You can buy gear in phases. Get parts that will work for either scenario.

DON'T CROSS THE STREAMS!

If you have to run a long XLR cable from your mic to your recorder, such as if you have a plant mic or if you are lucky enough to have a boom operator and you are the sound mixer sitting at an audio cart, remember to NEVER allow a cable carrying analog audio to run parallel to a power cable. Keep them away from each other if at all possible. If they must meet at some point, they must cross perpendicular to one another. If they do not, you will hear every bit of crackly, hissing electricity in your recording. Power and audio always cross at 90 degrees. End of story.

LIGHTS, DIMMERS, and BUZZING

Anyone who has swung a boom mic will tell you: lights make noise. The ballasts in fluorescent lights make a humming noise. High output production lights (HMI, Tungsten, and Halogen) will all give you problems if your mic or cable comes near them or their power cords or ballasts. In fact, any high-output electrical device such as a refrigerator will usually do the same. Avoid them like plague, and always make your AD unplug the fridge.

What's worse than all of those? Rheostats. Dimmers. And the lights attached to them. If there is a light fixture in the room you're shooting in that has a dimmer, chances are the DP will try to use it to help light the scene. But he won't like it turned all the way up, so he will use the dimmer switch on the wall to adjust it. If your mic comes anywhere near the dimmed light or the switch, you will hear a maddening buzzing in a frequency that will not go away no matter your filter settings. How do you remedy it? Convince the DP to either turn the light to full on, or off. Or keep the mic well clear of the area.

STATIC, WOOL, and SKIN

I mentioned previously having a fit of guilt over taping a wireless body pack for a lav mic directly to an actor's skin. Unfortunately, it was a necessary evil. The wireless transmitters I was using were susceptible to static interference. He was wearing a wool suit which, as it moved, was building up static charge and causing my transmitter to send only whooshing noises to the receiver instead of actual audio.

Having tried everything else I could think of to insulate the body pack from the wool suit, the only thing that worked was having the metal transmitter in direct contact with his skin while preventing contact with the wool. I taped it to his back, under his cotton t-shirt, with medical tape that I got from wardrobe. Even though he didn't have much hair on his back, I'm sure it wasn't comfortable removing the tape. Sorry, Chris.

10 INT. ON SET METHOD - DAY

So you have your kit assembled. You've made it to set on time, if not early (this is a must in this business), and all of your stuff is plugged in to each other and ready to roll. Right?

You've got your boompole rigged how it's comfortable, with the shock mount and blimp cradling the nice hyper-cardioid dialog mic at the end. Your cable is thick, well made, and well managed with quick release cable ties or gaff tape. Its solid XLR connector is plugged securely into both the mic and the field recorder, on input "1". Your headphones are connected to the recorder, any extra cable is wrangled, and you've adjusted the strap to fit snugly yet comfortably, just how you like it.

Be sure to allow some built in slack on both ends of your cables, so that an unexpected shift won't yank them out or, worse yet, damage your equipment or cable itself. I like to employ about a two inch loop just behind the connector at the recorder, secured with a soft tie-wrap, and I do the same at the headphone output jack when it's feasible. On the mic end, simply allow enough slack in the cable between the mic and the boompole that if the suspension mount tilts unexpectedly it won't damage the mic. Now that everything is connected, secure, and has some break proofing, what's next?

Power up! Don't wait on the director to ask if you're ready. That's the surest way to insure karma to deny you working batteries. Power up all systems and give the area a listen through the cans.

ADJUSTING HEADPHONE VOLUME

You will need to find a level that is comfortable to you. This is different for everyone or there wouldn't be a volume control on the headphone output and we would all simply listen to it at full recorded volume. Most people can't tolerate this and you shouldn't listen to it that loudly even if you can.

I like to set my phones at around 60-80% volume, usually, depending on the recorder. Some output louder than others. Be sure to choose a volume that is both loud enough for you to hear small details, yet low enough that: (a.) you don't hear a constant whirring hum when there is no real audible input (this is room tone/white noise), and (b.) you can tolerate it at that level all day without ear pain or a headache.

CAMERA JOCKEY
But why? I can just turn it down later if my ears start to hurt or a headache pops up. That's what the volume knob is for.

"Buzzzz!" Wrong! Your volume, once set, cannot change during your shoot. If it does your recorded levels will be different, regardless of what your level meters say. You must hear the sound consistently to be able to tell where the differences are. In time, with practice, you will learn to know what's good and what's not going to work; what to call a busted take, and what to ignore. If the volume you're delivering to your ears varies, you cannot make a consistent call on these issues. Find your preferred volume and lock it down. This is just as important as always using your own cans (chapter 7).

FEELING THE ROOM: PREVENTATIVE QC

No, don't walk around rubbing the walls. You have to feel out the room (i.e., use critical listening skills) to determine if there are any small noises in the area to avoid (see Chapter 3) and find workable fixes while there is time, prior to rolling camera. It's a pre-emptive strike, or Preventative Q.C., which you should definitely do!

Also at this point, be sure there are no hums, buzzes or crackles in your equipment. If a cable connection crackles when you swing the boom side to side, change that cable now! This is also the perfect time for a last minute battery check before things get crazy and you wind up getting the director's glare along with, "Waiting on sound!" as you scramble to get that safety screw out of the back of the recorder while you try to remember if you charged your spare battery.

Protect yourself from frustration and embarrassment. Do all of these quality and prep checks while the Grips are trying to figure out what the Director of Photography said. You have a few minutes. Use them well.

FILE NAMES and LABELING SCENES

So now you have all the prep done. Almost. The next step is to set up your recorder to benefit your post production team. Do this and they will love you. Don't do this, and they'll ask you to pour through the hundreds of sound files and log which file numbers go to which scenes and takes.

This is much, much, easier for everyone: Find the setting in your field recorder for "file names." Change the base file name to something meaningful instead of an arbitrary number.

Example: Your movie is called "Scratchy Hard Turtle" and you are about to shoot scene number 20 (consult the AD or director or script super to verify the scene number coming up if you aren't sure). Give the movie initials, add an underscore, and enter the scene number into the "file name" field. This would yield a file name as such: "SHT_20"

Now when you press record, your recorder will automatically create a file called "SHT_20_001" (typically, but not all will format it this way), which tells your dialog editor during post production that that file is for the film "Scratchy Hard Turtle," is associated with scene 20, and is Take 1. This should, if you coordinate with camera properly, mean that the editor can look at which picture take was used in the cut (in this case, 1), and read through the list to find your audio file for take 1 without having to listen through all the babbling and last minute discussions on the beginning of every audio take before someone finally slates the take and calls out which scene and take number the audio in that file should match.

The brilliant thing here is that every time the director calls "cut," you simply hit stop after camera operator has stopped rolling. The next time the camera operator hits record, so do you. Your recorder automatically assigns a progressive take number onto the end of the base file name every time you start recording a new file. You will end up with SHT_20_002, SHT_20_003, etc. until your day is done.

Just remember that every time the scene number changes, you must take the minute or less required and change the base file name, otherwise you'll have twenty takes of scene 25 labelled as takes 30-50 of scene 20 (as a random example).

Also, you can impress your post production crew even more by asking for sub scene headings to use. Such as, if the shooting script has been broken down such that scene 20 runs half a page and then they move to a separate conversation across the room as the scene progresses, and they've labelled that 20A, then just as you would a whole new scene, change your base file name to 20A, so that you have SHT_20A_001.

Organization is the key to post production going smoothly. Help that happen by staying organized on set. You'll give yourself a raise for it later.

"UM ... WOW THAT'S a LOT OF CRAP IN MY WAY"

So *now* you're ready! Lighting and grip is done. The camera is set. Focus marks are measured. Actors know their marks. The director is bouncing around behind the DP, itching to say *ACTION!* And you are ready. Ready to stick that boompole in there and … wait … where do you put the boompole when there is so much of that lighting and grip junk in the way? Why do they need four lights and two flags in a walk-in closet anyway? *Sigh…*

Finding the best angle to boom from can be tricky. One thing I learned from a great DP seemed so obvious after he said it.

"Behind the Camera is usually a pretty safe place to be." Well, yeah. You don't want to be seen, as the sound guy, by the camera. You don't want your mic to be seen by the camera. You also need a clear line of sight between all that lighting crap to stick your boompole and position the mic over the actors' heads. The camera needs clear line of site as well. If you are behind the camera, it cannot see you. The line between you (where the camera is located) and the actors will be unobstructed – typically – for you to insert your boom. It works. Usually. Well, it's just okay, is what it is. It's actually my last resort if I can't figure out something better. But, it is almost always a workable fallback position. So why is it not always optimal?

Often the behind the camera position restricts your movement. The overhead position of the boom sometimes needs to be tweaked during the take, especially if moving between two or more actors having a conversation. If you aren't able to have similar distance from the mic to the actors' mouths because you can't swing the boom the foot or two required, you have a problem. The audio will not be even and the natural reverb will be different for each actor's lines. This is not impossible to correct in post, but you shouldn't rely on "fix it in post." The better your production dialog sounds, the easier post process you will have and the better your movie will sound overall. Unless it's an ADR situation, forget "fix it in post" and start thinking "fix it in production" by modifying your boom position, angle, and technique.

That said, the **overhead boom** is still typically the optimal position for the mic. Keeping the mic 15-24" from an actor's mouth usually gives you that "sweet spot" where the full range of the voice is found, giving a warm, in-person sound without picking up too much ambient noise, reverb, and room hum. This overhead position doesn't always mean 90 degrees straight down, however. Sometimes you need to angle the mic from over the actor's shoulder or from slightly in front of his body. This especially is the case if you are flipping the mic back and forth between two actors as dialog progresses. If they are close enough to each other to keep both within that optimal distance from mic, keep the boom stationary as far as horizontal and vertical goes, and simply tilt the mic side to side as needed by twisting the boom in your hands. This requires special attention to hand technique, which I'll discuss shortly.

Now, what if you can't get the boom overhead no matter what you try? What if the lights are such a way that being overhead creates a shadow on the actor or background? What if the ceiling is low, and concrete, and creates an echo that your mic pics up too well when placed overhead? In that case, try **booming from underneath.** This is basically the same as booming from overhead, except, well, your mic is below the actor's mouth instead of above it. You get the same distance, the same full and warm voice, and the same reduced reverb and room hum. Everything is the same, just upside down. Oh and be sure you point the mic up at the actor's mouth instead of down at their shoes. This may seem obvious, but if I didn't say it, someone would write and complain that underneath boom made everything too quiet.

What if this still doesn't work? What to do when overhead isn't possible and underneath is still in frame? Time to get creative. Try a technique I call **shooting in**. You should be familiar with this because it's basically what you're doing whenever you have a camera-mounted microphone. The difference is that most camera mounted mics aren't as good as good boom mics (there are some exceptions, but few) and the distance becomes an issue. If you are shooting an exterior, shooting in isn't so bad because you can use a shotgun without adverse effects and increase your effective distance from the actors. Just be sure you aim well, like shooting a gun. Point that sucker straight at their mouths. If you are indoors, use a non-shotgun super-cardioid if you have one. If all you have is a cardioid, you can either crank the gain and hope it doesn't sound too bad, or put on a shotgun anyway and hope you don't get sizzle. Either way, it will be a gamble of whether or not you can match vocal tones, or if you're going to have to ADR the scene. Sometimes you can't avoid ADR.

"BOOM IN FRAME!"

If the camera operator keeps yelling at you to get the boom out of frame, congratulations, you're doing a great job keeping the mic close. However, if you keep doing it you're going to piss him off. The best practice here is to ask before the camera starts rolling where the edge of frame is located.

Simply asking, "Where's edge of frame?" while holding the boom where you want to have it is usually not an offensive question and can save everyone time by helping to keep you from busting takes by dipping your mic into the shot. Possible responses to this question:

- "You're barely in" or "You're way in," in which cases you should slowly move it away until you get the "all clear." Try to stay about three to six inches out of frame by visually marking your place against a point in the background. Keep the mic glued to that spot on the wall (by your perspective) throughout the take.

- "You're way out. Clear by a mile." In which case you follow up with, "Okay, how close can I get?" and move the mic closer until they yell "Stop!" Then back it out three inches and proceed as above.

- The third option you may get is an exasperated groan or sigh. In which case, your camera op is being a douche and doesn't care if you're in frame or how the audio sounds. In these situations I usually put the mic where I want it and let them yell at me to move it. Two can play the douchebag game.

By all means though, be professional and remember that what you're doing is just as important to the overall final product as what the camera operator is doing. Stand your ground and remind them of this if you are presented with option three. Just be nice about it, at first, or you'll continue to butt heads with douchebaggery.

CHECK YOUR STARTING LEVELS

Your position is set, frame found, room checked, refrigerators turned off, file names created, and you're ready to roll! Right? Almost.

Once everything is in place, before a new scene starts (don't do this between every take, that's annoying) ask the actors to run a couple of lines while on their marks. Be sure and specify "at scene volume" or they might just say their lines without being in character and wind up speaking way too low. In which case, when the scene starts, they will peak your audio and bust your take.

While the actors are running a couple lines for you, hold your mic where you plan to during the shot and check you level meters. Adjust the gain until they aren't peaking. If it's a dynamic scene with some yelling and some whispering, you will have a challenge during the take. My rule of thumb is: It's easier to turn things down in post than up, but it's also easier to deal with a little quiet than a lot of peaks and clips. A little soft on the volume can often sound smoother than too hot, and if you're having to choose between peaking or maybe being too quiet, go for maybe too quiet. Leave that limiter alone and off. Most of the time, non-adjustable limiters will cut out all of your audio for a quarter second after the peak they are eliminating, creating a hole in your dialog and screwing the take just as badly as a peak clip. Being that I've sworn to not get too technical in this book, I will refrain from explaining how to adjust a limiter if you have a recorder that allows it to be adjusted (usually only found on very expensive ones). Just leave it off and work with the gain control. You'll become a better sound recordist because of it, too.

All that said, these are your starting levels. Don't be married to them. They are just a best guess of what will work. Be prepared to adjust on the fly during the first take to get the best levels. You'll likely get a second take or three or four.

Another thing you can do when setting up your recorder to be sure and help your post audio people is to set your reference audio tone, if your recorder has it as an option. Without getting too technical here ...

The reference tone is something a recorder will automatically stick on the first second of your take. It puts out a 1 kHz tone at -20db (digital) so the post production dialog editor has a starting point for setting mix levels and knows how loudly your actors were actually speaking relative to the reference tone. If your recorder will do it, activate it. But be sure it's set to 1 kHz and -20db. If it isn't and you can't figure out how to adjust it in your specific recorder, just turn it off because it will be counterproductive.

"ROLL SOUND!"

Okay so now you're set. Ready to roll. It's your big moment. Your first take as a sound recordist on a movie shoot. The camera is in place, actors are on their "position 1" marks (where they will begin the scene), the director is ready, and ...

ASSISTANT DIRECTOR
Quiet on set! Roll sound!

You press the record button, place your boom carefully, settle in quickly, and call back to the A.D.,

YOU (SOUND MIXER)
Sound has speed!

A.D.
Roll camera!

CAMERA OP
Camera has speed!

No, you are not announcing methamphetamines in your pocket. You are telling the A.D. that your recorder is recording. Why do we say "speed" to indicate this?

It comes from the old days of recording on tape. When the wheels were turning on the recorder as it began recording, the statement that "sound has speed" meant that the tape was in motion. This is still the term used, even in digital world, because the statement "my red light is on" just sounds stupid. The same applies to the camera, of course – it's the old way of saying it from the days of shooting on film. Who does that anymore? Not people shooting on the cheap, that's for sure. Yet the terms remain.

Be sure to use this term at that moment on set, because if you say, "Okay" or "I'm rolling" or anything else besides "speed" or "sound has speed" or "sound is speeding," you will be revealing to the set that you are a noob. Your trust factor will drop dramatically. Maintain the "illusion" of being an experienced professional.

"BUST!"

Something everyone is always nervous to do is interrupt the take. Sometimes you shouldn't do it, regardless. Sometimes it's needed. How do you know when you should? This will largely come from experience, and learning what your director expects on each set.

Some standard examples of **when you should call the take a bust**:

- You have technical problems with your

equipment and either aren't recording after all, or aren't sure if you are or not. Meters not moving, or not hearing anything in your headphones; battery goes dead, memory card is full or stops working, or you start experiencing sudden inexplicable crackling noises during the take.

- A noticeable external noise is heard on top of the dialog and is persistent, such as a train, plane, or truck passing, or voices of crew or cast in another room, not in the scene.

Some examples **when to keep rolling regardless**:

- You notice the actors messing up their lines. You know it's not going to be a usable take, but there's nothing wrong with your audio, so it's the director's call on stopping the scene. You are not the director (unless you are), so as long as your audio recording is good, keep rolling.
- You accidentally dip boom into frame, and notice it. Often editing and/or your visual effects people can fix this, if it's only for a second. Watch your boom and shadows, but unless the camera operator or director stops the take because of your boom, just remove it from frame and keep going.

Point is, calling a "bust" on a take is serious business, especially when you're surrounded by a professional crew and cast. If it's you and three friends shooting a short, it's not as big of a deal. But learn when to say stop and when to keep on rolling.

STAY OUT of the WAY

Just like when you had to wait to figure out where you could stand and place your boompole until the camera and lights were set and you knew where the actors' marks were, you also need to stay out of the way of all that equipment and the people running it, before, during, and between takes. It's not that big of a deal. Just be courteous. By not being obstructive you'll help set efficiency, and the people you work with will respect you for it.

SET ETTIQUETTE

There have been whole chapters written but this boils down to a simple rule: Don't be an asshole. Be courteous and professional.

BOOM TECHNIQUE = HAND DISCIPLINE
A.K.A.
DON'T MOVE!

Now that you know how to choose and operate your equipment, how to not get kicked off of set, and how to position yourself to get the best sound possible, you need to learn how to keep *you* from being the reason you don't record good, clean dialog.

Rule number one with a boompole: When you're holding it, and sound is recording, do not move your hands. In fact, don't twitch a finger, lift a finger away from the pole, slide your hand down the pole, bump the pole against your own shoulder, or anything else that creates any vibration to the pole at all. All of these things will transmit a thump or bump type noise into the mic and you will record it, right on top of your best dialog take, regardless of how good your shock mount microphone suspension is.

Find where you are comfortable holding the boom and once you've settled for the take, stick to it. The surface of your hand becomes a part of the boompole. You can move the pole without your fingers or hands moving in relation to the pole. Trust me. I do it all the time. Practice this when nothing is going on, with the mic, recorder, and headphones on, so you can hear the tiny thumps I'm talking about. These will flat ruin your take because the only way to remove them from the dialog is with very precise and time consuming clip surgery in post-production.

11 SCENARIO LESSON 1
THE PERFECT INTERIOR

How should you set and use your equipment varies depending on the environment and type of shot. The first lesson: The "Perfect Interior."

Environment

What does that mean, to say it's perfect? You have carpet, heavy drapes over the windows, well insulated walls and ceiling, lots of well cushioned furniture, and the natural sound of the room is … almost nothing. It's dead. You notice no reverb when you speak. There is no noticeable noise from outside or elsewhere in the building. This creates a situation that is as near to perfect for recording dialog as you can possibly hope.

Microphone Selection

In this environment you could use almost any mic you want and it will sound good. To sound great, however, go with a nice cardioid or hyper-cardioid. Place it close, and hear how it's supposed to sound.

Recorder Settings

You don't need much sound alteration or trickery to make a perfect room sound nice, so don't restrict what you're capturing. Leave the gain soft, about mid-range likely, to avoid peaking. Leave the low-cut filter either off, or barely on. Try about 40 Hz with a 6 or 12db step cut. This will allow you to capture the full warmth of the actors' voices but still keep accidental thumps from being too obvious.

12 SCENARIO LESSON 2
THE "LIVE" INTERIOR

Environment

When a room is echo prone, or full of reverb, with hard wood or tile floors, not much furniture, no window dressings, and sparse of insulation in walls or ceilings, it is going to sound bad and uneven when you record in it. How do you handle this?

Deaden the room as much as possible using rugs, "sound blankets" (which are basically thick moving blankets that soak up some sound reflection when hung up on a wall), and if you have the ability to do so, use large chunks of foam in the corners to trap bass boom. If you aren't placing the blankets, rugs, and foam panels against the surfaces that are reflecting the sound to create reverb, you aren't going to have any luck. Cover as much of the offending surfaces as you can get away with, without the director laughing and trying to kill you. Also, be careful of gaff tape pulling paint and plaster off of the walls when hanging your blankets and such. Best option is to find a surface besides sheet rock or plaster to attach to.

Microphone Selection

In this type of room, you must ...MUST... use a smooth mic of the cardioid, hyper-cardioid, or super-cardioid variety. No shotguns. Ever. You must keep the mic close, with the gain turned low to mid. Also experiment with mic direction, avoiding pointing at walls and corners. If the floor is hardwood or tile, angle the mic to avoid direct reflection.

Another option, if you convince the director to do some super close up shots during the dialog takes, is to hang an omni mic on the boom, about forehead level, with the gain turned way down. This will cut out a great deal of ambient reverb and echo. With careful placement an omni lavaliere can also perform the same function, but the sound is never quite as sweet.

Recorder Settings

Gain being low means less power applied to your mic's signal, so the reception field area in effect seems smaller than it would be at higher gain. (In actuality, this is not what's happening to the microphone, but the effect is easier described in these terms than saying "the signal in path prior to the pre-amp stage circuit is weakened" and hope you know what that means.) This helps cut down the reverb. You can still – if using a mixer with a post-amp fader – bump the volume up.

[This is one of my personal tricks that most people don't know about and one of the things that make directors love my work, without knowing how I do it. Now you know how I do it, so you can be just as impressive. Just be careful you don't make the recordings too quiet. It takes practice.]

Think of "volume" and "gain" functioning as separate things. Gain is how much power and sensitivity you're applying to the mic signal, while volume is how *much* of that transmitted signal you are recording into your mix. Again, there are technical details that make this incorrect, but just roll with it.

NOTE: Volume and gain are actually interchangeable, from an engineering standpoint. It has to do with pre-amp, post-amp, which point along the signal path that it is affected by which amplifier, blah blah blah. But in terms of how the knobs and sliders on mixers and recorders with these labels actually affect and *behave* in your mix, keep them separated in your head. This will help you in understanding how to get a clean and smooth track recorded.

Here you should also utilize your low cut filter to help reduce reverb as well. It won't do much, but it can help. Slowly try higher settings (120 Hz, 160 Hz, etc., at -12db, -18db, -24db cuts) incrementally until you notice voices become tinny. Then back it off a notch.

13 SCENARIO LESSON 3
THE PERFECT EXTERIOR

Environment

Wow it's quiet. There's no traffic noise. No birds. Very little if any wind. The actors are standing still and not crunching leaves or gravel while they talk. There are no buildings around to create reflectivity of sound. It's perfectly quiet. That is, if it's daytime and your lighting guys aren't running a generator. If it's nighttime and there's a generator running the lights, you do not have a "perfect" exterior.

Microphone Selection

Here is the playground for a nice short to medium shotgun mic. You can actually, like the perfect interior, use almost any mic in this perfect exterior and it will sound good. But a nice shotgun will sound great and give you the ability to be a little farther away to take advantage of the setting for wider camera shots during dialog.

Recorder Settings

Again, you don't need much sound alteration or trickery to make a forest sound nice, so don't restrict what you're capturing. Just like with the perfect interior, leave the low-cut filter either off or barely on. Try about 40 Hz or 80 Hz with a 6 or 12db step cut. This will allow you to capture the full warmth of the actors' voices but still keep accidental thumps from being too obvious. If you have to move farther away from the actors, turn your gain up to keep their voices even but be aware you will also pick up more ambient and might need to adjust your low cut filter up a little, possibly to 80hz on a -12db cut.

14 SCENARIO LESSON 4
NOISY EXTERIOR

Environment

Traffic. Crickets. Gravel. Dry leaves. Wind. Lots of wind. More traffic. Passersby talking and yelling. So many noises can occur with exterior locations, especially those in urban or suburban areas, that it can be truly maddening for the sound mixer. Unfortunately, in these situations there is nothing you can realistically do to deaden or silence the ambient. Therefore, you have to work around it. Pull out the serious voodoo.

Microphone Selection

Shotgun! Mount up a nice, tight, longer shotgun. Encase it in a full blimp with full fuzzy wind attenuator ("dead cat") and rely on close placement with careful directionality to avoid noises.

If you're trying to avoid the crunching gravel under walking actors' feet, aim from the side to avoid the mic pointing past mouths to the gravel (as in overhead) or being too close to the gravel itself (as in underneath). Having a pistol grip shock mount makes this easier.

If you need to avoid cars passing or ambient conversations, get overhead and point straight down with perhaps a slight tilt away from the offending noise.

Alternately, as before with the noisy interior, this is sometimes an appropriate situation for a wireless lavaliere mic. Just be extra careful with placement if it's windy. Clothes make enough noise without throwing wind into the mix.

Recorder Settings

Here we have a situation similar to the noisy interior, only instead of ambient reverb and echoes, you're mostly trying to avoid ambient noise. Still, similar settings on the recorder will perform both tasks. Begin by keeping gain as low as possible with the mic very close to the actor's mouth. Then do the same routine with the low cut filter starting at about 80 Hz, -12db, and bumping it up until things sound crappy, then turn it back a notch. Obviously, if your problem is fixed before it starts sounding crappy, stop there instead.

15 SCENARIO LESSON 5
LARGE GROUP

Environment

Taking the previous examples of actual environment, whether good or bad and interior or exterior, having a large group of actors (which for a sound recordist means four or more) to record in a conversation presents special problems.

First step is to read the room or area and prepare for it as you would any other situation. Then, consider the actors. Are they going to be close together or far apart? Are they sitting around a small table or spread around a room? If they're spread around, the director will likely be taking close-ups of each. At that point you're in a single actor situation and it becomes much easier. If, however, you have a situation such as a game table with a medium or wide shot where the conversation happens without punching in close on each actor, you still have to get usable dialog tracks from each actor. Here's how:

Microphone Selection

On your boompole (or possibly multiple boompoles with multiple boom operators) mount up a good hyper-cardioid, cardioid or omni. Don't even bother with tight pattern super-cardioid and the like. You need something with smooth and even pickup on the off-axis angles, instead of something that makes the sound drop off when off axis. You need to be able to move quickly and sometimes only part of the way between actors and still have their dialog even in both volume and tone. Again, here is a good place for wireless lavs. However, don't rely only on those.

Always swing a boom.

Recorder Settings

Hopefully you have a good quiet ambient environment. To not have that in a large group situation compounds the difficulty and will make you seek out the bourbon before the scene is over. I once filmed at night in a city, outside in a gravel parking lot, with a fire pit burning, with six actors all having lines and moving around at the same time. I felt like I had truly achieved something when the dialog was all clear and the ambient could be covered with "room" tone. Whether loud or quiet environments, refer to previous lessons for how to set the recorder.

16 SCENARIO LESSON 6
WHEN TO SAY "NO"

This is a special section that addresses not how to record sound well, but how to know when you can't. It's often a very tough thing, especially for a new crewmember, to both know when he should say no and to actually do it; to tell the director or producer, "No, I can't record anything usable in this situation."

By studying this book, hopefully you have a better idea of what's possible and what's not when recording sound on location. By practice and experience you'll get to know the differences better and recognize those situations before you get started. If you go to the director and tell him it's not possible to get good sound in a particular shot, likely you will enter a conversation where you must explain why. Hopefully the director listens to you and either modifies the situation to help you record sound, or acknowledges that he will be sending his actors to the ADR studio. If not and he demands you record anyway, then do it. He will wind up in ADR regardless. But it will be worse if he winds up in ADR and you never mentioned that he would. He will say it's your fault, instead of knowing that you said it wouldn't sound good.

There's another situation where you need to stand your ground as well: When the director or producer tries to make your job too complicated because they think they know how it should be done. More often, it's their past sound failures making them tell you how to do your job. The paranoia and nervousness they experience is understandable but when they begin telling you to wire all actors at all times … no. (However, if you're working on a television show this is standard practice to avoid ADR when rapid turnaround times are needed) Assure them that for most situations the boom mic will sound better and if a situation arises where you see the need for wireless lavs you will use them. But otherwise they aren't necessary.

Always, always get room tone. I mentioned this previously but I will say again: your director and assistant director should be as adamant as you are about capturing room tone. If they aren't and want to blow on to the next scene and ignore your request for one minute of quiet … then they don't know as much as they think. Stand your ground and insist you get it or their post process will be awful. Make them hold the room for you. They will thank you later.

Your Diploma!

You are now a qualified sound recordist!

Maybe. Study and read through this book a few more times. Keep it with you on set for reference. Never assume you know everything there is to know about sound. Always seek out new information and ideas. Always keep learning. Make it a goal to learn something new on every set.

Good luck, have fun, and tell your friends that indeed,

Good Sounds Easy!

ABOUT THE AUTHOR

Jeremy F. Crowson began working as a production sound mixer when in his mid-thirties, after twenty years as a hobby and occasionally semi-pro musician. He always became the default sound mixer for whatever band he was in. Having acquired a solid background in both live sound and recording sound through music, he was approached to run sound for a short film production in 2010 by his friend Chuck Hartsell. After becoming hopelessly addicted to making movies as a result, Jeremy continued to study and experiment with location sound recording for movies. He also became involved with post production sound editing, sound design, Foley creation, and mixing. He has since worked as sound mixer and/or sound editor on multiple short films and 5 features, including production mixer for *Clubhouse*, winner of both Canada International Film Festival's "Award of Excellence in Filmmaking" for 2014, and Intendence Film Festival 2014 "Best Feature." He recently entered the world of producing, as one of the producers of *Red Season* (working title), an indie zombie-comedy feature. He is also currently writing a feature screenplay and is in pre-production and development of several feature films as producer through his company, Suncrow Productions.